Guided Journal

Belongs to:

_____

_____

_____

Suggestions for using Advice from a Tree Journal

Nature is a timeless and magnificient guide to help us in simple thoughtful ways. Through the beauty of the trees we can remember and reconnect with the joys of life, growth, personal achievement, as well as our own health and well being.

Trees are an amazing gift!
They are the great teachers simply by reflecting and living their true nature! An oak is proud to be a beautiful oak! It doesn't spend energy trying to be an aspen! In simple ways trees remind us to be the beauty of ourselves!

Often as we remember our favorite tree
or tree experience, wonderful feelings and memories may arise within us. The experience of reconnecting with *our* roots can be enriching and helpful in living our highest and truest nature. Perhaps you may want to journal about your tree experiences or other gardening, hiking or walking nature experiences.

Twelve of the journal pages have a line from the Advice from a Tree poem. On the *Stand Tall and Proud* page, and blank pages that follow, pehaps you might make notes about ways that you feel good about yourself or ideas for how you might stand taller and prouder. The *Think Long Term* pages invite you to list your goals and aspirations and steps in achieving them. For the *Drink Plenty of Water* pages record your thoughts about ways to nurture your strength and health.

Use the pages of this journal however you like. Perhaps you may want to use this tree journal as a way to harmonize your own cycles and seasons with those of nature. Write, draw, paste your favorite pictures... most of all have fun!

I think I'll "leaf" you to the joys and discoveries of your journaling. And never forget ... "*you're* tree-mendous!"

Ilan Shamir

By Ilan Shamir

Published by Better World Press, Inc
P.O. Box 272309
Fort Collins, CO 80527
http://www.yourtruenature.com
email: IlanShamir@yourtruenature.com

Thanks to the trees for their gift of paper!
Printed on Recycled Paper

We participate in the 100% Replanted program.
Tree seedlings have been planted in a protected watershed area
by the non-profit organization Trees, Water & People
for all paper used in the printing of this journal.
Visit http://www.ReplantTrees.org

Story of Advice from a Tree

It was one of those difficult days . . .
one of those days that tore at the very roots of my being. I just
had to get outside to breathe and somehow find a way back to my
center, a return to the peace and clarity of my soul. I managed to
open the front door and with tears in my eyes, I began to move
along the sidewalk, lifting one foot in front of the other without a
clue where I was going. Exhausted, I leaned against a huge
Cottonwood tree; the deep ridges of the bark held me close. I said,
"I've been working for you for many years now, planting thousands
of trees, teaching about the miracles of the earth and now I need
your help! Can you help me? I need some advice." I felt the tree
reach out to me, to wrap me in its branches, to comfort me as I
leaned against its steady trunk. This old and wise Cottonwood tree
spoke to me with clarity and wisdom. I felt hopeful, renewed, loved
and went home and word for word wrote
the following caring message
from this tree friend . . . .

Dear Friend,
Stand Tall and Proud
Sink your Roots deeply into the Earth
Reflect the Light of your true nature
Think long term
Go out on a Limb

Remember your place among all living beings
Embrace with joy the changing seasons
For each yields its own abundance
The Energy and Birth of Spring
The Growth and Contentment of Summer
The Wisdom to let go like leaves in the Fall
The Rest and Quiet Renewal of Winter

Feel the wind and the sun
And delight in their presence
Look up at the moon that shines down upon you
And the mystery of the stars at night
Seek nourishment from the good things in life
Simple pleasures
Earth, Fresh Air, Light

Be content with your natural beauty
Drink plenty of water
Let your limbs sway and dance in the
breezes
Be flexible
Remember your Roots

Enjoy the View!

Dear friend . . .

Stand tall and proud!

Sink your roots deep into the earth

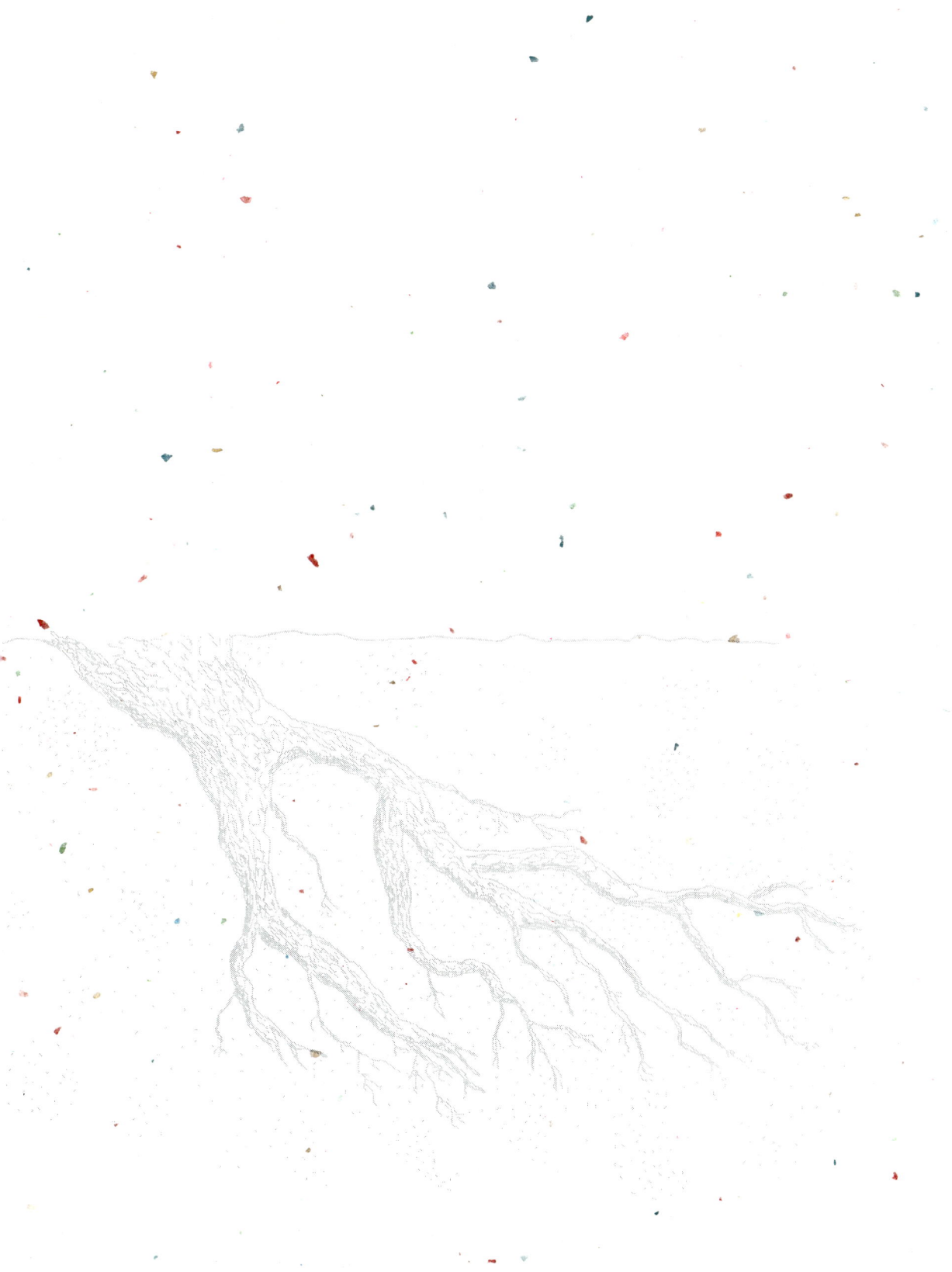

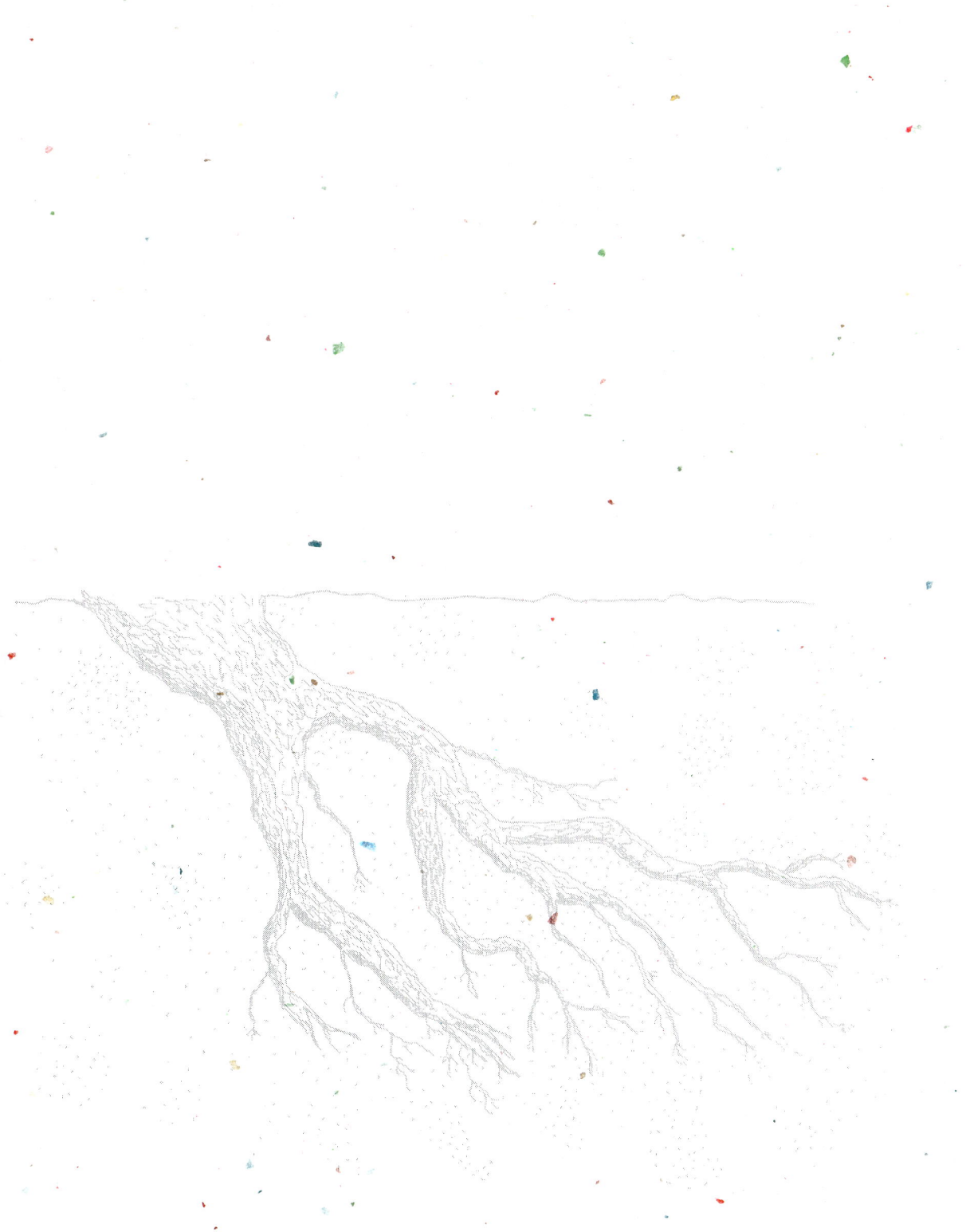

Reflect the light
of your own true nature

Once a very old man
was planting trees.
Someone came up to him and said,
"Why are you planting trees?
You will never be around
to see them mature."
His reply was simple,
"I do not plant them for myself,
I plant them for future generations!"
. . . As a child he had so much
enjoyed the magnificience
of the trees that had been planted
years before that he wanted
to show his appreciation
and give the earth
his own special gift.

Think
long
term

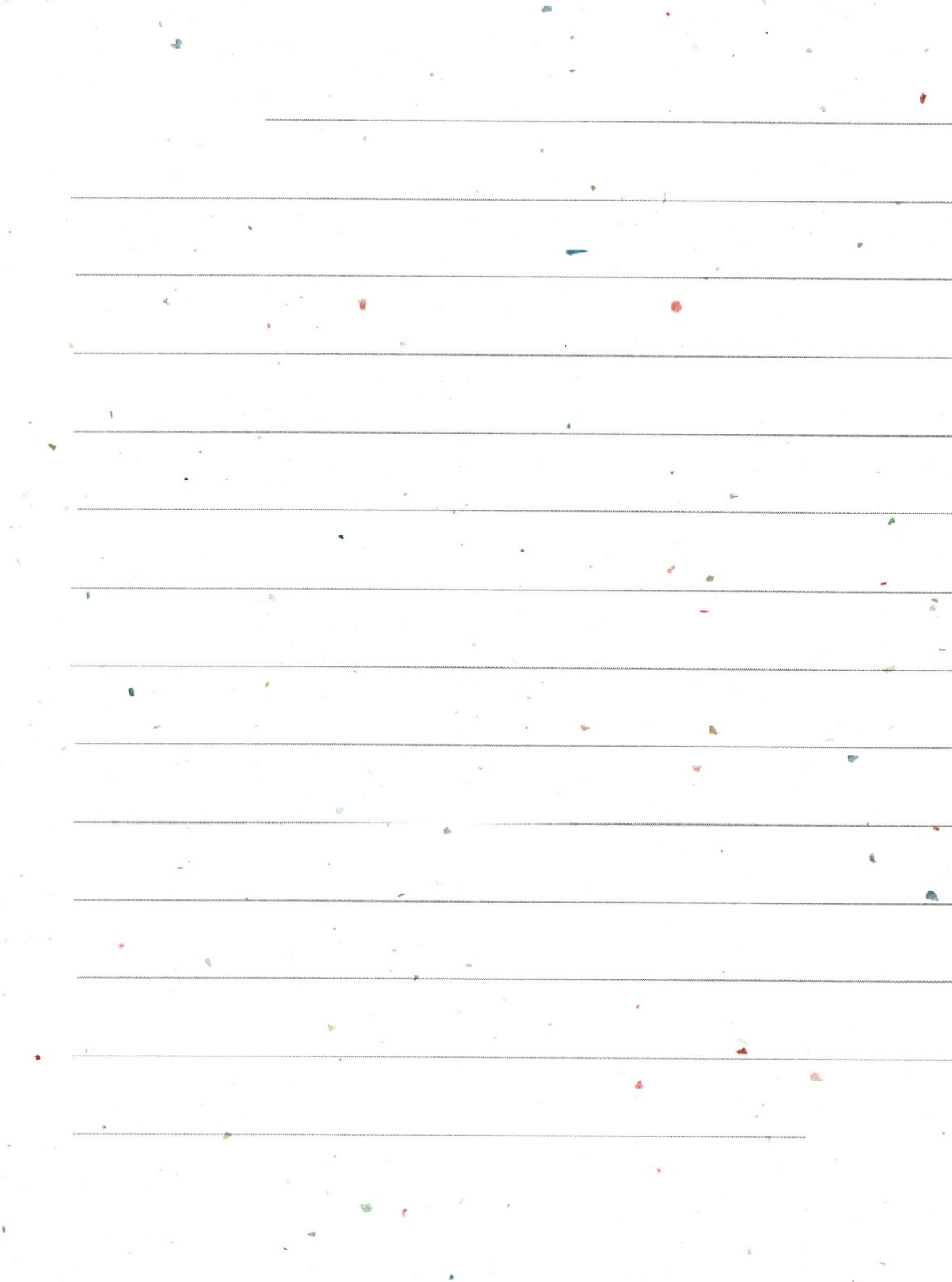

Go out on a limb

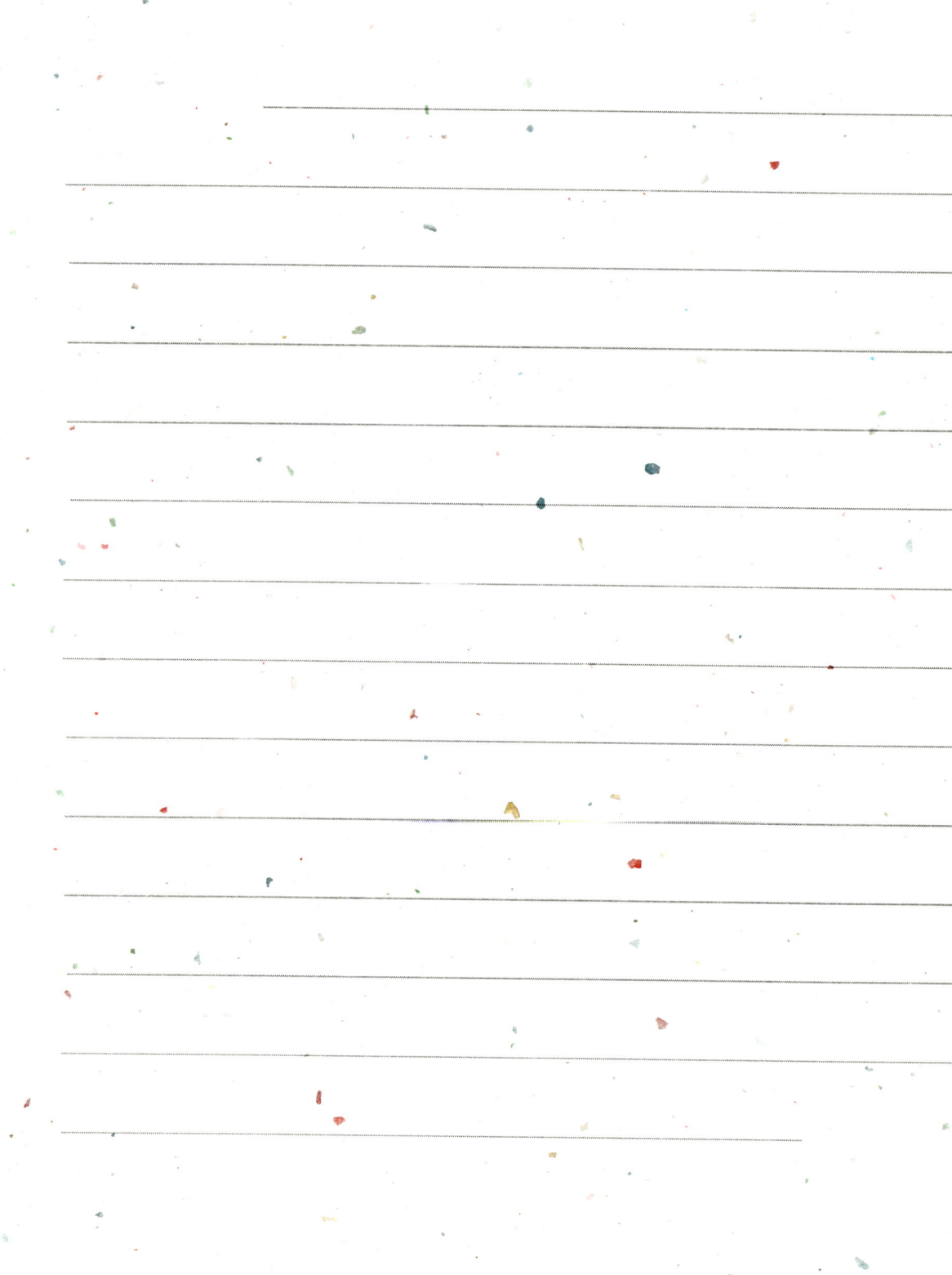

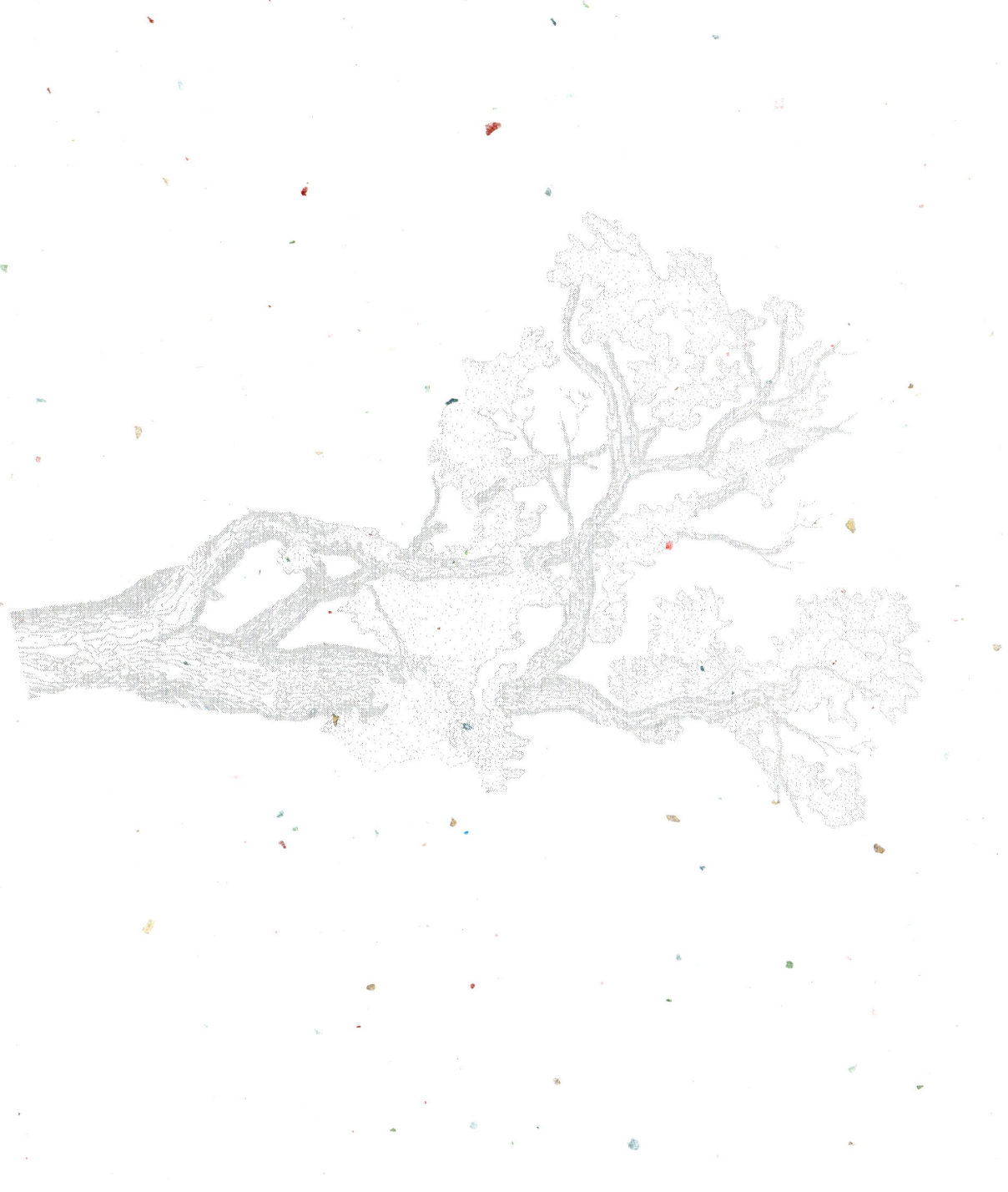

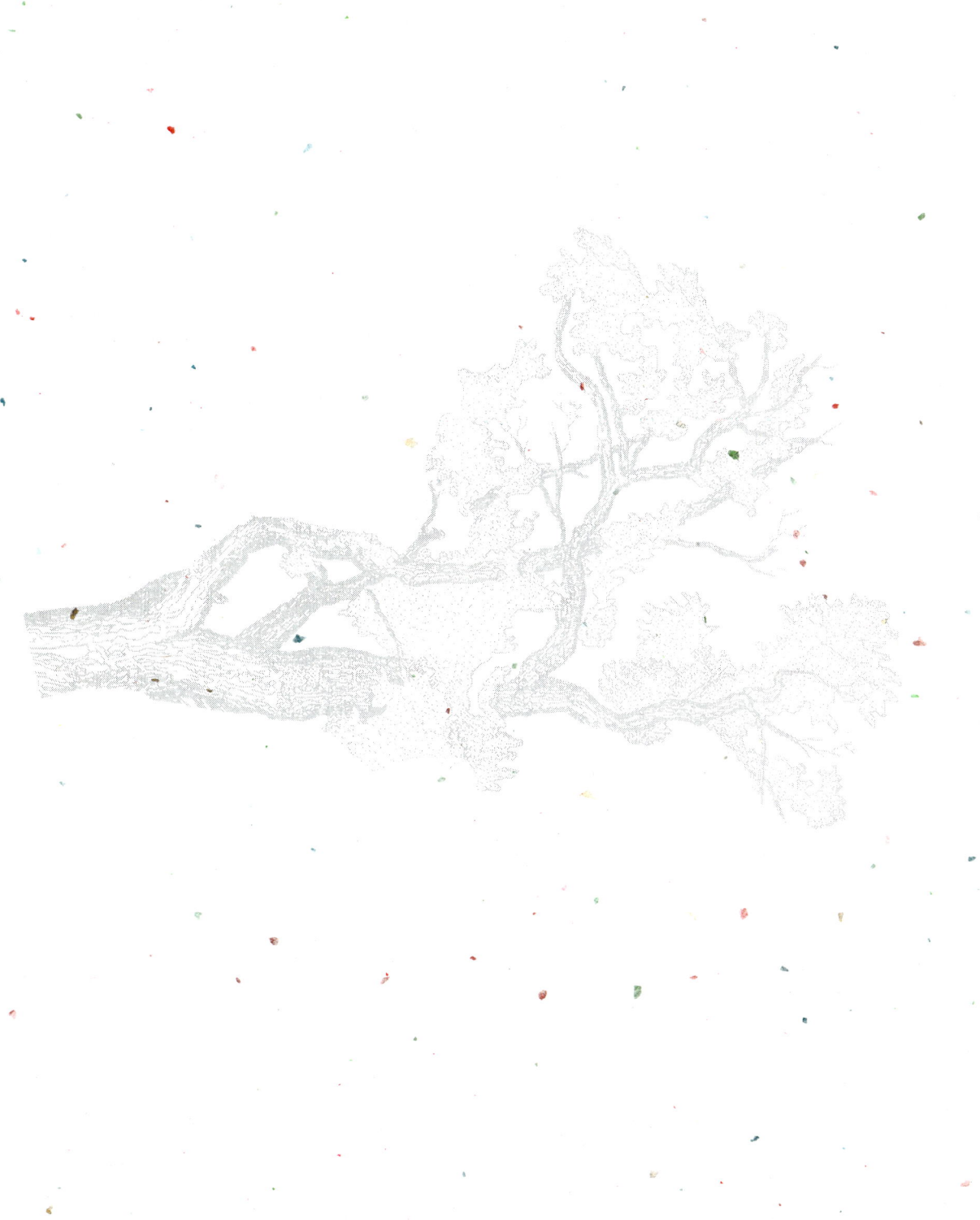

Remember your place
among all living beings

Embrace with joy
the changing seasons . . .

For each yields its own abundance

The energy and birth of Spring

*The growth and contentment
of Summer!*

The wisdom to let go . . .
like leaves in the Fall

The rest and quiet renewal of Winter

Feel the wind and the sun
And delight in their presence
Look up at the moon that shines down upon you
And the mystery of the stars at night
Seek nourishment from the good things in life
Simple pleasures
Earth, Fresh Air, Light

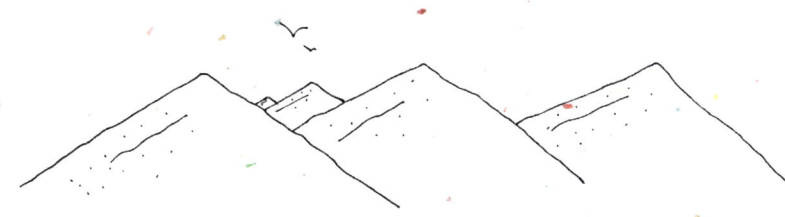

Be content
with your   natural beauty!

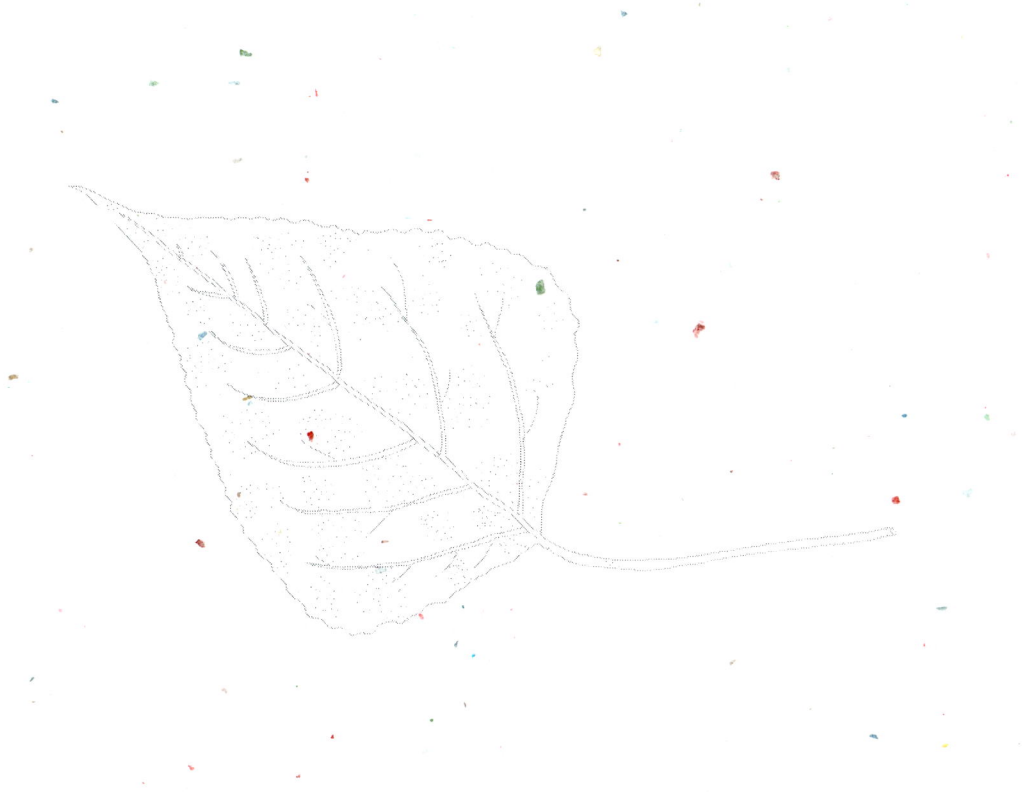

Drink plenty of water

Let your limbs sway and dance
in the breezes

Be flexible

Remember your roots!

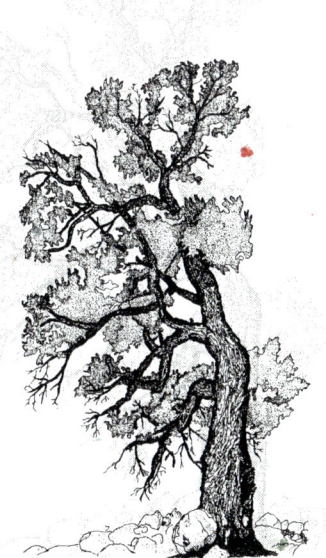

Enjoy the view!

Ilan Shamir

Advice from a RIVER

Advice from a MOUNTAIN

Advice from a GARDEN

Advice from a TREE

Your True Nature

Keynotes & Workshops

Ilan has been featured in NPR's All Things Considered, Good Housekeeping, The L.A. Times, The Wall Street Journal, The Washington Post, The London Journal and over 100 other print and broadcast media worldwide for his unique products and programs.

For booking and product information visit www.YourTrueNature.com or call 1-800-992-4769

A lasting gift for someone special and the Earth!

"The Gift of a Tree"

1 Your purchase price of $8.95 for one tree, or $18.95 for a three tree grove, pays for the planting of an 18" to 24" tree(s) by the non-profit organization Trees, Water and People (an audited 501c3 organization), for the person and occasion you choose. Current planting area is the Magdalena protected area in El Salvador. This project was recently featured on National Geographic Discovery Channel. Mahogany, Cedar, Cocao and other native tree varieties are planted and cared for.

2 You receive a kit for each tree you purchase which contains a gold embossed greeting card for you to send to the person you are planting a tree for. A postcard is also included with the kit which you return to us to initiate the tree planting.

3 Both you and the recipient can view the tree planting location, nursery and communities that plant the tree on the Your True Nature website! A lasting gift to someone special and

It's Easy as 1,2, TREE!

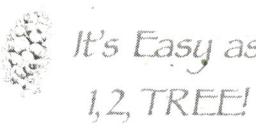

Order Form

QTY	QTY	QTY	OCCASION
1 Tree	6 pack	Grove	
$8.95 ea	$42. ea	$18.95 ea	Cards do not
___	___	___	**Birthday**
___	___	___	**Memorial**
___	___	___	**Holiday**

Also visit our website at www.YourTrueNature.com for more information and pictures

All Occasion
Good for:
Friendship, Birth, Anniversary, Wedding, Graduation, Congrats, Father's Day, Mother's Day, and Thank You

> **Special DISCOUNTS:** Order six pack and Price is $42.00 for 6 cards. (Save $1.95 per card)

Your Name _____
Address _____
City/State/Zip _____
Email _____
Telephone _____

Total Qty _____ at $ 8.95 = $ _____
Total Qty _____ at $18.95 = $ _____
Total Qty _____ at $42.00 = $ _____
CO res. add 2.9% sales tax $ _____
Shipping $ 6.50
GRAND TOTAL $ _____

Enclose check or order online:
Your True Nature, Inc.
Box 272309, Ft. Collins, CO 80527, (800) 992-4769
Email us at: grow@yourtruenature.com.
Order online at **www.YourTrueNature.com**
Visa and MC credit cards accepted online or at our 800#